Floating Lanterns

Also by Mercedes Roffé from Shearsman Books

Like the Rains Come: Selected Poems (1987-2006)

Mercedes Roffé

Floating Lanterns

translated
from Spanish
by
Anna Deeny

Shearsman Books

First published in the United Kingdom in 2015 by
Shearsman Books
50 Westons Hill Drive
Emersons Green
BRISTOL
BS16 7DF

Shearsman Books Ltd Registered Office
30–31 St. James Place, Mangotsfield, Bristol BS16 9JB
(this address not for correspondence)

www.shearsman.com

ISBN 978-1-84861-372-0

Original poems copyright © Mercedes Roffé, 2009.
© Bajolaluna, 2009
Translations copyright © Anna Deeny, 2015.

The right of Mercedes Roffé to be identified as the author
of this work, and of Anna Deeny to be identified
as the translator thereof, has been asserted by them
in accordance with the Copyrights, Designs and Patents Act of 1988.
All rights reserved.

Acknowledgements
Originally published in Argentina in 2009
by Bajo la luna, Buenos Aires.

Cover photo:
Photograph of the 2008 Annual Lantern Floating,
used by permission of Shinnyo-En, Hawaii, and
Na Lei Aloha Foundation. All rights reserved.

Things that leave us speechless: Mercedes Roffé's *Floating Lanterns*

> *In the beginning there was Goodness.*
> *And from it, all things.*
> Epilogue, *Floating Lanterns*

Mercedes Roffé (Buenos Aires, 1954) is one of Argentina's most important and internationally recognized contemporary poets. Her works include *Poemas* (1977), *El tapiz* (published under the heteronym, Ferdinand Oziel, 1983), *Cámara baja* (1987; 1996), *La noche y las palabras* (1996; 1998), *Definiciones Mayas* (1999), *Antología poética* (2000), *Canto errante* (2002), *Memorial de agravios* (2002), *La ópera fantasma* (2005; 2012), *Las linternas flotantes* (2009) and the volume of selected works, *Milenios caen de su vuelo* (2005). *Mansión nocturna*, a second volume of collected works, is forthcoming from Monte Ávila in 2015. Among other distinctions, Roffé was awarded a John Simon Guggenheim Memorial Fellowship in poetry (2001) and, more recently, a Civitella Ranieri Foundation Center residency fellowship (2012). Roffé lives in New York City and is the founding director of Ediciones Pen Press.

When *Las linternas flotantes* was published in 2009, Mercedes Roffé explained that the book was "a reaction to things that left us speechless: September 11, Argentina's economic debacle that led to long months of national and individual hardship and incertitude, the tsunami, Hurricane Katrina, and so many things that seemed to come together in just a few years, things that were so disastrous for the whole world."[1] Like Jeremiah, the prophet of the *Book of Lamentations*, who mourns the destruction of Jerusalem through the use of acrostics, dirge and communal lament, Roffé, of Sephardic Jewish origins, attends to these "things that left us speechless" through elegy and meditation. In Hebrew, Jeremiah's biblical text is called *Eicha*,

---

[1] Conversation with Mercedes Roffé, Manhattan, 2009.

(איכָה,'êkâ), which means "alas" and "how." An exclamation of grief's unwieldy dimensions along with the need to grapple with its perplexing causes, *eicha* is the sentiment that grounds *Las linternas flotantes*. And for Roffé, like the prophet, poetic forms hold the unique capacity to engage these sentiments and ask *how* such catastrophic events come to happen.

But September 11, 2001, Argentina's crisis that same year and Hurricane Katrina in 2005, were ultimately no worse than the other Latin and North American disasters that preceded them. Roffé, who moved to Manhattan in 1995, had lived through her country's Dirty Wars (1976-1983), in which anyone identified as a "subversive" was targeted by a series of military juntas. Tens of thousands of individuals—pregnant women, children, labour and political leaders, doctors, Jews, clergy, students, human rights activists and intellectuals—were detained, tortured and "disappeared".[2] Indeed, just when young Spanish writers were emerging hopeful from over thirty years of Franco's military regime, a wave of coordinated dictatorships, supported by the United States and its economic allies, swept through much of Latin American in the 1960s, '70s and '80s. Poets from the Southern Cone such as Mario Benedetti (1920-2009), Juan Gelman (1930-2014), María del Carmen Colombo (b. 1950) and Raúl Zurita (b. 1950), to name only a few among many, searched for language techniques that might speak as much to the local, immediately apparent atrocities, as to the hemispheric conditions that either made such atrocities possible or managed to circumvent their forces. While one of Roffé's earliest texts, *Cámara baja*, addresses the ethical urgency of those years, it was the timing of this recent series of events that incited her to focus on evil, *el mal*, as that which precedes and even undergirds economic, political, religious, scientific or natural explanations for catastrophes. But how do we speak of things that come before language and actually foreclose our use of it?

---

[2] See CONADEP report at http://www.desaparecidos.org/nuncamas/web/index2.htm.

Roffé sought language registers and techniques evocative of creation myths, sacred texts, philosophy and poetry that meditates upon human nature and our propensity for evil.[3] She brings together Buddhism, Tibetan Yoga, the Judeo-Christian Bible, the Kabbalah, Plato's *Republic*, T.S. Eliot, Beat poetry—particularly that of Anne Waldman—the oral traditions of Medieval Spain and Native North American cosmogonies. What binds these diverse materials is Roffé's use of anaphora. Note, for example, the effects of "To sleep" and "To inhabit" in this opening poem:

> To sleep with eyes wide open
> To sleep alert
> Standing, forehead propped against the day's hinge
> *To inhabit the night wholly in the pure   presence of the letter*
> Aleph   Beth   Yod
> the mark   the trace-cipher
>
> To inhabit the night entirely in vigil
> To inhabit the night wholly insomniac
> To inhabit life wholly wakeful
>
> *because to feel is more than seeing but even more so is to merge*

Anaphora emphasizes meaning in the repetition of a word or concept. However, as each word is repeated, it lets meaning go, allowing the word to materialize in such a way that it bears sound more fully. Thus, we are moved from the word as something that signifies a particular or many concepts, to the word as sound, a relationship that fuses the materiality of the utterance with our own bodies. This is how anaphora creates tension that underscores the individual letter sounds—the building-blocks of language—at the same time that it foregrounds the promise of meaning. Through anaphora Roffé thus recalls the process of

---

[3] Transcript of "Oh mentida joya, la palabra," Esther Ramón and Pilar Fraile's interview of Mercedes Roffé on *Definición de savia*, Radio Círculo, Círculo de Bellas Artes de Madrid, February 24, 2010.

language building in the face of destruction. When catastrophes level cities, bodies and our loved ones, language too is leveled in our screams. Nonetheless, as Susan Gubar has suggested, poetic techniques can remind us of our subjective capacity to construct language again. They offer the possibility, or at least the hope, that a broken language, and from there the broken body, might also be remembered whole even if it is never to be recuperated.[4]

This first poem draws on Tibetan Dream Yoga, which teaches that one way to sleep is to remain in constant vigil, the idea being to achieve illumination. Here too are the first, second and tenth letters of the Hebrew alphabet: Aleph, Beth and Yod. Yod, (י) the smallest letter, recalls the geometry of creation in its script; it is also the unit, or atom, from which all other letters, and thus things that might be named, begin and end. Yod is the extraordinary contradiction of the origin, the presence of God in all things in that it signals its own vast potential at the same time that, like an infant, it is the tiniest and most humble of all the letters. In this dream state, illuminated, Roffé then moves us to the "suspension of sense" or "sentido" as a univocal concept, toward "fullness" as necessarily plural. "[F]ullness" levels the privileged sense, which is sight, with the aural, olfactory, tactile and gustatory, again, grounding the experience of meaning in the body.

> Suspension of sense to see fullness
> Suspension of sense to hear fullness
> Suspension of sense to smell and touch
> taste of fullness
> Suspension of sense to feel fullness
> Suspension of all senses for the fullness of sense
>
> The multiple and singular
> The untranslatable

---

[4] See Susan Gubar, "The Long and the Short of Holocaust Verse" in *New Literary History*, Vol. 35, No. 3 Critical Inquiries, Explorations, and Explanations (Summer, 2004).

The echo
   perfect and full

It is only through this embodiment, dream-illumination, suspension, fullness, and inhabitation at the edge of language that we might prepare to face the existence of evil indexed in poem II.

In Asian religious ceremonies, floating lanterns convey the living's longing for the dead as they illuminate wandering the horizon, the edge of water and sky, night and day, sleep and wakefulness. But each individual lantern reflects a more profound call for unity among the living. We are like those lamps wandering and searching for one another at those very edges. Similarly, Walter Benjamin believed that all languages yearn for one another in the common things they wish to express. That is, languages crave a prelapsarian, pre-Babelic unity. Roffé also expresses this need for confluence by presenting sacred, philosophical, poetic and meditative traditions that have complementary, if not corresponding, impulses. *"[B]ecause to feel is more than seeing but even more so is to merge"* suggests a common longing for unity in a world that has been so deeply wounded and torn apart.

I don't know what the language—those terms, contracts, sanctions, ideologies, governments or diplomatic strategies—of such a unity would look like, nor, it seems does anyone. But what Roffé asks is how we might provide a human response to that predicament without perpetuating the terms of the disaster in the first place. In poem IV, Roffé speaks to that ironic and catastrophic perpetuity:

3000 bombs
3000 bombs
3000 bombs in one weekend
how many faces
how many hands
how many legs
how many veils-gauze stuck to skin burning

how many stones over stones torn away
how many lives torn from life

Roffé's response to this sense of continual loss is *Las linternas flotantes*, a prayer of human poetic craft destined for human—not divine—ears. This prayer seeks a subjective agency over what she considers history's master narratives, narratives that have made us their object:

> I think that humanity is a victim—today as in the Middle Ages and in Biblical times—of certain discourses that consider themselves "masters" (that of science, politics, religion, economy, that of the mass media...). Half of those discourses, so rigorously articulated, are intentionally false; they're deceitful. The other half is and has always been simply wrong.
>
> I think of poetry and art in general as an alternative to that monolithic idiocy, that is so sure of itself, inviolable—until history or reality reveals them as pathetic, temporary constructs. Unfortunately, those constructs cost many lives. Arrogance and idiocy always cost lives... I think of poetry as a tentative discourse that is always on the side of life and peace. Always.[5]

Roffé thus identifies evil as that which incites such master narratives at the same time that it conserves them. Poetic form, as a

---

[5] From "El poema como eco de un universo musical," interview with Nelly R. Guanich, *Periódico de poesía* No. 44, de noviembre de 2011. "Como te digo, creo que la humanidad es víctima —hoy como en la Edad Media y en los tiempos bíblicos— de ciertos discursos que se pretenden "maestros" (el de la ciencia, el de la política, el de la religión, el de la economía, el de los medios...). La mitad de esos discursos, tan rigurosamente articulados, son intencionalmente falsos, mentirosos. La otra mitad son y han sido siempre sencillamente erróneos. Concibo la poesía y el arte en general como una alternativa a esas necedades monolíticas, seguras de sí mismas, infranqueables —hasta que la historia o la realidad las pone en evidencia como tristes, temporarios constructos. Lamentablemente, esos constructos cuestan muchas vidas. La prepotencia y la necedad siempre cuestan vidas... Pienso en la poesía como un discurso tentativo, pero del lado de la vida y de la paz. Siempre." My translation.

"tentative discourse" is, like Yod, as humble as it is ambitious, as multiple as it is persistent in its desire to build again, to recover, and remember that even *before* evil and language there was goodness.

ANNA DEENY
Washington, D.C.,
2015

Floating Lanterns

I.

Dormir con los ojos abiertos, bien abiertos
Dormir alerta
Dormir de pie, con la frente apoyada en el vano del día
Residir la noche toda en la pura   presencia de la letra
Aleph   Beth   Yod
el rasgo   el trazo-cifra

Residir la noche entera en la vigilia
Residir la noche toda insomne
Residir la vida toda en duermevela

porque sentir es más que ver y más aun es fundirse

Residir la noche en el velo de la noche
Residir la noche toda en el alba
Residir la noche toda en el alba pura y plena
Residir la noche en el umbral de la noche
Residir la noche entera
del otro lado del sueño

Residir la noche en el mar profundo
en la vigilia del mar
Residir la noche toda en lo profundo
y ver la noche toda reflejada en la noche
y el fluir de los peces cortando a pique el cielo
el canto de los peces cortando el cielo
y las lustrosas yemas de las algas cimbreando
            punteando
la noche oscura del agua

I.

To sleep with eyes wide open
To sleep alert
Standing, forehead propped against the day's hinge
To inhabit the night wholly in the pure   presence of the letter
Aleph   Beth   Yod
the mark   the trace-cipher

To inhabit the night entirely in vigil
To inhabit the night wholly insomniac
To inhabit life wholly wakeful

because to feel is more than seeing but even more so is to merge

To inhabit the night in the veil of night
To inhabit the night wholly at dawn
To inhabit the night wholly in the pure and full dawn
To inhabit the night at the threshold of night
To inhabit the night entirely
on the other side of sleep

To inhabit the night in the sea deep
within the sea's vigil
To inhabit the night wholly in the depths
and look at night wholly reflected in night
and the fish stream cleaving the sky
their flanks splitting the sky
and the lustrous fingertips of swaying algae
          tapping
water's dark night

los mascarones fantasmas de los buques del sueño
los mascarones   en el aire azul flotando
         maridándose con las almas

Residir la noche en el borde de la noche
abajo, donde mora el reflejo verdadero
más allá, donde mora la luna,
no su reflejo
sino su cara de plata verdadera

Tejer la noche con el alba, el alba con el día
el día con el estridor del despertar
las trompetas del día
los metales vibrantes de la orquesta del día

Residir en la llama, en su bóveda azul fría,
en el vibrante azul inofensivo
refugio, templo, iglú en el origen del fuego
estar en el centro y verlo
estar en el centro y hablarle
estar en el centro y no temer
y que no sea temible
sólo belleza pura
oro
y poder verla de frente y verla
y que no sea temible aunque lo sea
SUSPENSIÓN
de todo,
de todos los sentidos
de lo corpóreo y frágil, vulnerable, mortal, hirsuto
de todos los sentidos

the ghostly figureheads of slumber's ships dream
the figureheads   in blue air floating
            wedding souls

To inhabit the night at the edge of night
below, where true reflection dwells
beyond, where the moon dwells,
not its reflection
but its true silver face

To weave the night with dawn, the dawn with day
the day with the stridor of awakening
the day's trumpets
the vibrant metals of its orchestra

To inhabit the flame, its cold blue dome,
the vibrant innocuous blue
refuge, temple, igloo at the origin of fire
to be at the center and look at it
to be at the center and speak to it
at the center and not fear
and that it not be frightening
only pure beauty
gold
and to be able to look at it and see it
and that it not be frightening even though it is
SUSPENSION
of all,
of all senses
of the corporeal and fragile, vulnerable, mortal, hirsute
of all senses

Suspensión del sentido para ver lo pleno
Suspensión del sentido para oír lo pleno
Suspensión del sentido para oler y tocar
gustación de lo pleno
Suspensión del sentido para sentir lo pleno
Suspensión de todos los sentidos para el sentido pleno
Lo múltiple y uno
Lo intraducible
El eco
    perfecto y pleno

Porque hay verdad y hay ecos
Hay verdad y hay sombras
Hay verdad y hay la flagrante arquitectura
    que la cubre y la oculta y la rodea
    y la mina y la cerca y distorsiona
Hay verdad y hay espejos
Hay verdad y hay espejos que la cercan
Hay verdad y hay espejos
    que traen del sueño la rama que lo prueba
Y hay verdad y hay espejos
    que desdicen
        hasta los rosados dedos de la aurora

Suspension of sense to see fullness
Suspension of sense to hear fullness
Suspension of sense to smell and touch
taste of fullness
Suspension of sense to feel fullness
Suspension of all senses for the fullness of sense
The multiple and singular
The untranslatable
The echo
        perfect and full

Because truth and echoes exist
Truth and shadows
Truth and the flagrant architecture that
      covers it and conceals it and surrounds it
      and mines and encircles and distorts it
Truth and mirrors
Truth and mirrors that encircle it
Truth and mirrors
      that from dreams convey the branch of evidence
And there is truth and there are mirrors
      that unsay
      even the rosy fingers of dawn

II.

Hay maldad
    Residamos al borde de la noche
Hay corrupción y mentira
    Residamos al borde de la noche
Hay mezquindad, malicia, engaño, alevosía
    Residamos a la vera del día
Hay pobreza y dolor
    Residamos a la vera del día

Residamos la noche a la vera de la noche
Residamos la noche en el seno urgente del día

Hay mal, hay fraude, hay sombra
Moremos
    en el estallido del día
Moremos
    en el seno de la noche
    en el fétido seno del mal   contra el mal

II.

There is wickedness
    Let us inhabit the edge of night
Corruption and lies
    Let us inhabit the edge of night
Cruelty, malice, deception, treachery
    Let us inhabit the verge of day
Poverty and pain
    Let us inhabit the verge of day

Let us inhabit the night at the verge of night
Let us inhabit the night in the urgent bosom of day

There is evil, fraud, shadows
Let us reside
    in the day's shatter
Let us reside
    in the night's bosom
    in the fetid bosom of evil   against evil

III.

No hay distancia
la distancia es fuego
No hay distancia
la distancia es humo y cenizas
la distancia es espejo
es la tierra que pisas
la distancia es mi rostro en el espejo
tus pasos sobre tus pasos
sus cenizas sobre tus cenizas

No hay distancia
Soy ella
soy la insomne
      la reencontrada maltratada en el desierto
soy sus ojos
soy su espejo
soy su distancia de mí y de sí misma

No hay distancia, hay ceguera
No hay distancia, hay reencuentro
No hay distancia, hay distintos colores de desiertos
mares   de distintos colores
hierba   cielo   noche
del color distante del tiempo

No hay distancia, hay colores
hay desiertos

III.

There is no distance
the distance is fire
No distance
it is smoke and ashes
it is reflection
it is the earth you step
this distance is my face in the mirror
your steps on your steps
her ashes on your ashes

There is no distance
I am she
I am the insomniac
      the one found again persecuted in the desert
I am her eyes
her mirror
her distance from me and from herself

There is no distance, there is blindness
There is no distance, there is reunion
There is no distance, there are different desert colors
seas   of different colors
grass   sky   night
of the distant color of time

There is no distance, there are colors
and deserts

Hay casas y hay escombros
hay casas allanadas y casas demolidas
hay tiendas, hay iglús, hay tepes
hay lofts hay búnkers hay palacios
hay ranchos hay taperas hay ramallah hay veneno hay títeres
    hay soplones
hay las siete ciudades de oro y el oro de los incas
oro en polvo   oro negro   oro
por aquellos que somos y no somos
oremos
digamos la oración, la palabra que falta
la cifra   el número   la clave
residamos la noche en la pura presencia

porque sentir es más que ver y más aun es fundirse

hay que volver
hay que volver atrás
hay que volver atrás hacia delante
hay de desovillar la madeja del tiempo
hay que volver al futuro
hay que volver a la masa azul noche estrellada
donde éramos luz
minúsculas partículas de luz dispersa
en el seno de la noche
hay que volver
hay que desovillar la trama de esta noche

There are houses and rubble
houses raided and demolished
tents, igloos, teepees
lofts   bunkers   palaces
there ranches huts there ramallahs venom puppets
      snitches
there are the seven cities of gold and the Incan gold
gold dust   black gold   God
bless us and those who are not us
let us pray
let us speak the prayer, the missing word
the cipher   the number   the key
let us inhabit the night in the pure presence

because to feel is more than seeing but even more so is to merge

We have to return
we have to go back
we have to go back forward
unwind the skein of time
return to the future
we have to return to the blue mass starry night
where we were light
miniscule particles of light dispersed
in the bosom of night
we have to go back
unwind the weft of this night

Disolvamos la noche
Respiremos
Un soplo
Insuflemos de luz la noche   de aire
Insuflemos la noche de noche verdadera

No pasarán
No pasará esta noche
No pasará esta noche por el ojo de una aguja
No pasarán
los títeres los embalsamadores los escupidores
escupitajos   esquirlas
de podredumbre
No pasarán
roña y sudor
             armado
hasta los dientes

fauces
ratas
despojos portadores de despojo
infección portadora de infección

Cuzco   Tíbet   Bagdad

Y esto caducará también.
No el mal. No el mal.
Sólo los nombres.

Let us dissolve the night
Let us breathe
One breath
Let us infuse the night with light   with air
Let us infuse the night with true night

They will not pass
This night will not pass
This night will not pass through the needle's eye
They will not pass
the puppets the embalmers the spitters
spit   shrapnel
of rottenness
They will not pass
scab and sweat
              armed
to the teeth

jaws
rats
spoils carriers of spoil
infection carrier of infection

Cuzco   Tibet   Baghdad

And this too will pass.
Not evil. Not evil.
Just the names.

IV.

Sueña el grano que ya es espiga dorada
y sueña el niño que es hombre
sueña el mal que pasa inadvertido
y el bien que juega una partida y gana
Sueña el rocío que ya es el mar profundo
y la pepita de oro que es fíbula y ajorca
La raíz sueña que es rama, que un pájaro hace nido en ella
y la nube que es lluvia ya y que penetra la fresca
aspereza de la grama

Un álgebra superior
equipara
el día y la noche
lo que será y lo que ha sido
lo que vendrá y el origen
sereno de las cosas

tumulto y paz
convulsión y mar calma
la realidad se ofusca en el retorno
vórtice-tiempo
vórtice
donde se arrebuja el alma

Hela ahí,
la Realidad
la Joya
el velo de cristales sobre la cara

IV.

The kernel dreams it is already a gold spike of corn
and the boy dreams he is a man
evil dreams it passes unnoticed
and goodness that it plays a hand and wins
The dew dreams it is already a deep sea
and the golden seed that it is a brooch and armlet
The root dreams it is a branch, that a bird makes its nest in it
and the cloud that it is already rain and seeping the fresh
asperity of grass

A superior algebra
equates
the day and night
what will be and what has been
what will come and the calm
source of things

tumult and peace
convulsion and sea soothed
reality is bewildered upon the return
vortex-time
vortex
where the soul is bundled

Here it is,
Reality
the Jewel
the veil of crystals over the secret

recóndita de las cosas   su hora naciente
Sol
vórtice-luz
vórtice-palabra
vorágine suspendida
disolución
disolución

3000 bombas
3000 bombas
3000 bombas en un fin de semana
cuántas caras
cuántas manos
cuántas piernas
cuántos velos-vendas pegados a la piel ardida
cuántas piedras sobre piedras arrancadas
cuántas vidas arrancadas de la vida

trace of things   its nascent hour
Sun
vortex-light
vortex-word
suspended maelstrom
dissolution
dissolution

3000 bombs
3000 bombs
3000 bombs in one weekend
how many faces
how many hands
how many legs
how many veils-gauze stuck to skin burning
how many stones over stones torn away
how many lives torn from life

V.

Porque el Ángel vigila.
Vela.
Alerta está sobre un costado del hombre.
Ángel-lechuza.
Sutil está.
Ve sin ser visto.
Trabaja.
Los ángeles trabajan.
A veces
una bala perdida los hiere
—primero a ellos—
luego se abre camino y mata.

Ángel dormido.
Desvaneciente.
Ala herida.
Gotas de sangre-alma.

Vigila.
Vela.
Alerta.
Sutil está
sin ser visto.
Sobrevolando el hilo de la vida.
Sutil el hilo
el ala.
Transparencias.
Nervaduras de aliento-vida
Sombra blanca sobre tierra blanca
contra blanco muro de agua transparente.

V.

Because the Angel keeps vigil.
Watches.
Alert standing over one side of man.
Angel-owl.
There subtle.
Seeing without being seen.
Working.
Angels work.
Sometimes
a stray bullet wounds them
—first them—
then it finds its way and kills.

Sleeping Angel.
Fading.
Wing wounded.
Drops of soul-blood.

The Angel keeps vigil.
Watches.
Alert.
There subtle
unnoticed.
Flying over the thread of life.
Subtle the thread
the wing.
Transparencies.
Veins of life-breath
White shadow over a white earth
against a white wall of transparent water.

Crece el jazmín y se abre
en su blanco bienoliente.
Vida sutil   el Ángel se corona
de blanco bienoliente y se abre
jazmín alado a un costado de tu hombro.
Vida sutil.
Susurro
       de aguas transparentes.

Música es
aquello que bendice.
Silencio bendecido y coronado
       de gotas bienolientes.

Cristal del mundo
Cristal-aleph que encierra —libre—
todo lo que debía haber sido
todo lo que, en algún lugar, (se) es.
Lugar otro, devenir de lo exacto-destinado.
La vida es el sueño de un ángel
herido en su costado,
en su ala
       transparente y perfecta.

Un desvío fatal: interferencias
de un susurro-silencio transparente y perfecto
—un jazmín abierto y entregado.

Jasmine grows and opens
in its sweet-scented whiteness
Subtle life   the Angel crowns itself
of sweet-scented whiteness and opens
jasmine winged at one side of your shoulder.
Subtle life.
Whisper
     of transparent waters.

Music is
what blesses.
Silence blessed and crowned
     with sweet-scented beads.

Crystal of the world.
Crystal-aleph that encloses—free—
everything that should have been
everything that, in some place, (one) is.
Another place, becoming of the exact-destined.
Life is the dream of an angel
wounded on its side,
on its wing
     transparent and perfect.

A fatal diversion: interferences
of a whisper-silence transparent and perfect
—an open and willing jasmine.

Las flores son infinitas. No en número.
Cada una.
Cada una un roce de lo otro en esta vida.
De una orilla en la otra.
Reminiscencia.
Emanación primera de la Primera
Emanación
      —transparente y perfecta.

Cada cual a su flor.
Cada cual a su aliento.
El Ángel vela
herido en su costado.

¿A qué herida atender
primero?
¿a qué llaga, a qué laceración
para parar la sangría
de un mundo herido
en todos sus costados?

¿En qué estrella de cristal radiante
atesorar su suspiro, su sangre
blanca-transparente sobre la tierra-muro blanca
herida
de esta sombra blanca diferida siempre
siempre en otro lado
moribundo siempre
herido siempre y entregado?

Flowers are infinite. Not in number.
Each one.
Each one the touch of the other in this life.
Of one shore in the other.
Reminiscence.
Initial emanation of the First
Emanation
          —transparent and perfect.

Each one to her flower.
Each one to his breath.
The Angel watches
wounded on its side.

Which wound do we attend
first?
which sore, which laceration
to stop the bleeding
of a world wounded
on all sides?

In which radiant crystal star
should we treasure its sigh, its blood
transparent-white over the world-wall white
wounded
of this white shadow deferred always
always elsewhere
always dying
always wounded and willing?

VI.

La luz se hizo.
¿Quién ha de dudarlo?
Y los pastos y los cielos y los mares.

Sutil aquel que separó
el azul del azul
el día de la noche
el verde metálico del atardecer
del verde-vida del prado.

Vida sutil.
El Ángel vela
herido en su costado.

Brutal.
Brutal también.
¿Quién podría negarlo? ¿Quién
dudará que hay
              sangre
mucha
sangre
murano derramado
por la tierra-muro blanca sombra
oh muro-mundo siempre
herido
siempre
perfecto   henchido
en el cristal-aleph de un devenir

VI.

And there was light.
Who could doubt this?
And the fields and skies and seas.

Subtle the one who divided
blue from blue
day from night
the dusk's metallic green
from the life-green of the meadow.

Subtle life.
The Angel watches
wounded on its side.

Brutal.
Brutal also.
Who could deny it? Who
would doubt that there is
                          blood
so much
blood
murano shedding
throughout the world-wall white shadow
oh wall-world always
wounded
always
perfect   swollen
in the crystal-aleph of a becoming

silencioso y perfecto
                    siempre
en otro lado?

El Ángel-Número.
Cifra perfecta, infinita, feliz
concatenación
de aleatoriedades
—sin origen ni fin.
Ochocientos billones de blancos
pétalos bienolientes tiene
el jazmín de lo real
—abierto y entregado.
Emanación del loto originario
—partícula
        de blanca fe.

Jazmín-noúmeno.
Sinergético loto
de ocho y tantos billones
de pétalos bienolientes,
heridos y entregados.

¿Qué fue antes:
el loto o el jazmín?
¿Por qué caminos vamos
si hay camino
—tiempo herido en su costado?
¿Hay antes y después?
¿Sendero hay?

silent and perfect
                         always
elsewhere?

The Angel-Number.
Perfect cipher, infinite, happy
concatenation
of randomness
—without beginning or end.
Eight hundred billion white
sweet-smelling petals have
the jasmine of the real
—open and given.
Emanation of the first lotus
—particle
    of white faith.

Jasmine-noumenon.
Synergetic lotus
of eight and some billion
sweet-smelling petals,
wounded and given.

What was before:
the lotus or jasmine?
Through which paths do we go
if there is a path
—time wounded on its side?
Is there before and after?
Is there a way?

Hay un aleph-cristal perfecto
ensangrentado.

Completud de tallas convergentes hay
y en el centro el vacío.

There is a perfect aleph-crystal
bloodstained.

Integer of convergent cuts there are
and at the center emptiness.

VII.

He llegado hasta aquí.
A la herida del ala.
Contradicción perfecta
donde todo es posible
donde todo danza su danza-vórtice
de silencio y vacío.

La luz apenas
juega a deslumbrarnos.
A idear las formas que nos guían
rotundas e ilusorias
        —mesa, silla, espejo... : rama del paraíso...
rama
del sueño en la vigilia
—abierto y entregado.

No entres por ahí.
No acerques tu mano tibia y trémula
al dorado picaporte.
Verás la escena que te fue destinada
—precisamente aquella que debías
ver y no ver.
Tu Alejandría siniestra y familiar.
Roma bombardeando la casa de tu infancia.
Una Babel de mutismos.
No entres.
No abras los ojos.

VII.

I have gotten to this point.
To the wing's wound.
Perfect contradiction
where everything is possible
where everything dances its dance-vortex
of silence and emptiness.

Light barely
plays to dazzle us.
To make out the forms that guide us
definitive and illusory
      —table, chair, mirror… : a branch from paradise…
a branch
from a dream in the vigil
—open and given.

Do not go in through there.
Do not place your tepid tremulous hand close
to the golden latch.
You will see the image that was destined for you
—precisely the one that you should
see and not see.
Your sinister and familiar Alexandria.
Rome bombarding your childhood home.
A Babel of mutisms.
Do not go in.
Do not open your eyes.

Desnudeces.
¿Quién dice cuerpo?
¿Quién dice eros o amor?
Ágape
      interrupto en su descenso.

Todo vuelve.
Como aquí,
todo vuelve.
¿Pero a qué?

Oh loto bienoliente salpicado
de sangre y barro.
Escombros, miembros, esquirlas, ojos
infectando
el sagrado
      estanque de la vida
su corriente sagrada y estancada
en una fosa común.

En las paredes de la caverna,
entre estalactitas de sangre y barro, esquirlas y miembros cercenados,
un jazmín proyecta su sombra blanca trémula.
Oh jazmín bienoliente y perfecto,
abierto y entregado.

Nakedness.
Who says body?
Who says eros or love?
Agape
 interrupted in its descent.

Everything returns.
Like here,
everything returns.
But to what?

Oh sweet-smelling lotus sprayed
with blood and dirt.
Rubbish, limbs, splinters, eyes
infecting
the sacred
 pond of life
its sacred and stagnant stream
in a mass grave.

In the walls of the cavern,
among stalactites of blood and dirt, splinters and severed limbs,
a jasmine projects its white tremulous shadow.
Oh sweet-smelling and perfect jasmine,
open and given.

VIII.

Caída no hubo.
Ni Hombre ni Mujer primeros.
Ni aciago Demiurgo.
Ni un Dios dormido y sordo, cabeceando
en su silla raída.
Nuestro sueño es su siesta.
No nosotros.
Aquel que se contrajo   Aquel que
se replegó sobre sí
nos ungió en la lumbre.
Expiración de amor sí somos.
Obra-hijos de un momento febril de inspiración
              —y de un miedo profundo.

Caída no hubo. Hay
multiplicidad de vilezas.
La palabra del necio
La mirada torva de la envidia
La vara del poder
La cuenta enrarecida del avaro
Las pústulas de la avidez
El botín sin fondo del amor fingido

Pero caída no hubo. Hay
              desde el origen
partículas de excrecencias acres, fétidas
como un ícor de Dios. Eso sí.

VIII.

There was no fall.
Nor first Man or Woman.
Nor ill-fated Demiurge.
Nor a God asleep and deaf, bobbing his head
in a worn chair.
Our dream is his repose.
Not us.
He who contracted   He who
went to himself
anointed us in the firelight.
Expiry of love is what we are.
The work-children of a febrile moment of inspiration
                              —and a deep fear.

There was no fall. There is
an abundance of wickedness.
The word of the fool
The grim look of envy
The rod of power
The avarice's rarefied accounts
The blisters of ambition
The endless spoils of feigned love

But there was no fall. There are
                           from the beginning
particles of acrid excrescences, fetid
like the ichor of God. This yes.

Pero caída no hubo.
Somos aún ese alba.
Centelleante y oscura.

Somos el sueño de una nena exhausta
la noche de la fiesta.
Somos la noche de la fiesta.
El lado oscuro de un palacio
engalanado hasta los dientes.
Bufón e ilusionista somos.
La cosa
y el falso halo de las cosas.
Acaso el halo
          verdadero y palpable
de una evasión
sin retorno.

Todo vuelve.
Todo.
¿Hacia qué?

Hacia un jazmín que se pudre amarillento en el mal olor de un vaso.
Hacia un loto final y terco
que persiste
en exhibir su mugre.

Ese vaivén.
Esa duda que insiste
somos.
Esa esquirla clavada en el costado
del ángel que nos guarda.

But there was no fall.
We are still that sunrise.
Glittering and dark.

We are the dream of a girl tired out
on the evening of revelry.
We are the evening of revelry.
The dark side of a palace
adorned to the hilt.
We are the joker and illusionist.
The thing
and the false halo of things.
Maybe the halo
                real and palpable
of an evasion
without return.

Everything comes back.
Everything.
Toward what?

Toward a jasmine that rots yellow in the foul smell of a glass.
Toward a final and stubborn lotus
that persists
in exhibiting its grime.

That oscillation.
That doubt that insists
we are.
That splinter pierced into the side
of the angel that guards us.

IX.

Entonces...
si era todo mentira
si —es cierto—
era todo mentira...
Entonces:
podemos asistirnos.
Presenciarnos.
Un pacto no pequeño.
(¿Qué más darse?)

El instante
que agota los sentidos
no agota una verdad.

Y sin embargo
morir un poco
ver la cara de Dios,
irse o venir, le dicen
¿de dónde? ¿a dónde?
De una ladera a otra.
De una cima a una sima.
O de lo bajo alzarse a lo profundo.
De lo uno a lo Uno.
De la noche a la luz sin fuente conocida.
Del instante a la suspensión
del tiempo
y al olvido de un sí
abierto y entregado.

IX.

Then…
if it was all a lie
if—it is true—
it was all a lie…
Then:
we can assist each other.
Being there.
Not a small pact.
(What more can we give of ourselves?)

The instant
that depletes the senses
does not deplete a truth.

And yet
to die a little
to see the face of God,
come or go, as they say
from where? to where?
From one hillside to the other.
From one summit to an abyss.
Or from the lowly rise to the profound.
From the one to the One.
From the evening to light without a known source.
From the instant to the suspension
of time
and to the forgetting of oneself
open and given.

¿Puede ser tanto error?
¿No será todo, uno y lo otro?
¿Uno y todo
           el camino hacia lo otro?

Could it be such an error?
Would it be all, one and the other?
One and everything
          the path toward the other?

X.

Todo destino es escándalo
Todo destino en su
    extrema vulnerabilidad
    su desnudez
    su escorzo
    su violencia
es escándalo
    de luz y desazón

X.

All destiny is a scandal
All destiny in its
    extreme vulnerability
    its nudity
    its torsion
    its violence
is a scandal
        of light and discontentment

XI.

¿El amor será al cuerpo
lo que la contemplación al alma?
¿Ese sosiego?
¿Esa intuición
            del todo en el instante?
¿Ese relámpago en el que
lo real se revela
acorde con su eco?
¿La suspensión fugaz
que presiente todo,
y todo lo comprehende?

¿Será aquel hiato en el fluir del tiempo
el único hogar y patria verdadera?
Hogar y patria:
            Llamo así al poseerse,
al mirarse y verse reflejado
en un agua
confiable y serena.
Cuerpo de luz
Cuerpo de bien
Hiperbólico pétalo bogando
entre una y otra ribera.

¿Y si no son dos las riberas?
¿Si todo es uno?
¿Si no son dos ni uno
sino un glisando de espejos
hacia y desde la luz   —o el fango?

XI.

Would love be to the body
what contemplation is to the soul?
That stillness?
That intuition
          of every thing at an instant?
That bolt of lightning in which
the real is made evident
in accord with its echo?
The elusive suspension
that perceives and
comprehends everything?

Is that pause in the flow of time
the only true home and homeland?
Home and homeland:
              This is what I call to possess each other,
as you look at each other and see your own reflection
in trustworthy and serene
water.
Body of light
Body of goodness
Hyperbolic petal rowing
between one shore and the other.

And if there are not two shores?
If all is one?
If there are not two or one
but a glissando of mirrors
toward and from the light   —or the mire?

Cada estación con su afanoso demiurgo
más confundido que cruel
obnubilado, hundido
en el exceso
de un reino que ignora y que lo ignora.

Regente, príncipe y niño —todo a un tiempo,
todo a destiempo.

¿Y si no fuera todo más
que un viaje
por las edades congeladas de ese príncipe
hacia la luz   —o el fango?

Each station with its diligent demiurge
more confused than cruel
deadened, sunken
in the excess
of a kingdom he ignores and that ignores him.

Regent, prince and child—all at once,
all untimely.

And if it were nothing more
than a voyage
through the frozen ages of that prince
toward the light   —or the mire?

XII.

Ésta es mi alma
Ésta es mi luz
Éste es mi soplo en ti
Éste, el hálito de luz entre mi mano
y la punta de tus dedos
en el abrazo primero en el cuenco de mi mano
Redondel
Esfera es
el abrazo ése que me excluye
Esfera-Tierra Prometida
Esfera-patria y memoria de la patria
de la que todo me expulsa y me destierra

Esfera-origen y fin
Esfera-estrella y brújula y lazarillo
y una luz en el centro.

Ésta es mi alma
Éste mi soplo en tu soplo.
Centella de lo que solo existe
en la vasija que eres
Vasija iluminada
Vasija numinosa
Vasija-cofre de Pandora y boca de la serpiente.
¿Qué mayor comunión?
¿Qué más darse?

XII.

This is my soul
This is my light
This is my breath in you
This, the waft of light between my hand
and the tip of your fingers
in the first embrace within my cupped hands
Rondure
It is a sphere
the embrace that excludes me
Sphere-Promise Land
Sphere-homeland and the memory of homeland
from which all things exile and banish me

Sphere-origin and end
Sphere-star and compass and blind man's guide
and one light in the center.

This is my soul
This my breath in yours.
Scintilla of what only exists
in the vessel you are.
Illuminated vessel
Numinous vessel
Pandora's vessel-safe and mouth of the serpent.
Is there a greater communion?
What more can we give of ourselves?

Ésta es mi voz en ti
Éste, mi aliento reificándose
en el vacío: la pura Ausencia
—un azul flotando sin sustancia
sobre la cual posarse—
las partículas de mi voz quebrándose
(¿Pero cuál? ¿qué partícula exacta
de mi voz en ti?)

(¿Y si jamás se retrajo?
Si jamás
 se replegó sobre sí
y estamos aún sin ser
 en el misterio de su vientre?
Pero...
¿vientre y cabeza y mano tiene
Aquel que es El que es?)

Lo Perfecto se excluye.
Cerrado sobre sí
—su bien, su mancha
lo reintegra y lo niega.

This is my voice in you
This, my breath reifying itself
in the emptiness: in the pure Absence
—a blue floating without substance
upon which to rest—
the particles of my voice breaking apart
(But which one? Which certain fragment
of my voice in you?)

(And if He never withdrew?
If He never
       drew back on Himself
and we still were without being
              in the mystery of his belly?
But…
does The One That Is have
a belly and head and hand?)

What is Perfect retreats.
Closed on itself
—its goodness, its stain
restores and denies it.

XIII.

En la semilla está el árbol
y el hombre y la mujer,
en la sangre gomosa de su madre.
En la estrella, la vida
según se hizo posible
y en la palabra, la idea que se ignora,
aquello que se oculta y se devela,
aquello que se grita
y promulga en lo callado.

En la partida se dibuja el mapa minucioso del destino
y recoge la llegada, una a una,
las migajas de pan que jalonaron
las diversas estancias del camino
        —albas y noches
        grutas y llanos
        el recoleto silencio
            el tenebroso
        y la estentórea música
        de una risa
        que se creía olvidada.

Todo está allí
        —aquí—:
lo múltiple en lo uno
y en lo uno
ese segundo infinito contenido
        que se desgrana en el tiempo.

XIII.

Within the seed is the tree
and the man and woman,
in their mother's viscous blood.
Within the star, life
as it became possible
and in a word, the unknown idea,
what hides and discloses itself,
what is screamed and
decreed by the unspoken.

Upon leaving the meticulous map of destiny is drawn
and gathers the arrival, one by one,
the bread crumbs that marked off
the different dwellings along the way
              —dawns and nights
              grottos and plains
              the secluded silence
                    the dark
              and the stentorian music
              of a laugh
              that was thought forgotten.

Everything is there
        —here—:
the multiple in the one
and in the one
that infinite second restrained
            threshed over time.

XIV.

Ese hueco en el alma
ese hueco en la bóveda del cielo
ese cañón de luz
    cruzando la creación
    de arriba abajo
    como un iris, un puente, una promesa.

O más —¿a qué iluminarlo
    de un oro, un siena, un cadmio
    que tal vez nadie vio
    que tal vez fue sólo su modo de nombrarlo?

:

la nada plena
la suspensión total
en el dorado seno de todo lo creado

un hiato
        contundente y fecundo
Esa ausencia absoluta
    —lugar de encuentro.

Tú en la guerra
Tú en la miseria
Tú en la opulencia
Tú apedreador

XIV.

That hollow in the soul
that hollow in the sky's dome
that canyon of light
    intersecting creation
    from the top down
    like an iris, a bridge, a promise.

Or more —why illuminate it
    with a gold, sienna, cadmium
    that perhaps no one saw
    that was perhaps the only way of naming it?

:

full nothingness
total suspension
in the golden bosom of all that was created

a pause
        resounding and fecund
That utter absence
        —the place of encounter.

You in war
You in misery
You in opulence
You who stone others

Tú constructor de casas
Tú que sales cada día a prodigar tu parte de mentira
    en la cierta mentira necesaria
Tú que insistes en que busquen tu nombre
        en el registro de lo humano
Tú que buscas o finges que buscas
        un nombre que no encuentras

You, builder of houses
You who go out each day to lavish your share of lies
    in that certain necessary lie
You who insist your name be searched
              in the human registry
You who search or pretend to search
        a name you do not find

XV.

El poema es el rostro en el espejo
más verdadero que el rostro y que el espejo.
El poema es el flujo de la sangre
                    más allá del cuerpo,
el ritmo de la sangre más allá de la sangre
—sus cauces rigurosos, su latido sordo y unitario.

El poema es el ritmo de lo otro en mí
más allá de mí, siempre, más allá,
donde mi silencio se topa con tu ritmo
y repercute en mí, que solfeo en el poema
un ritmo numinoso,
cifra que hace eco en el eco
que es cuerpo verdadero
—lo numinoso en ti y en mí—
el ciclo de las esferas tocándose y abandonándose
—alejándose, sí, una de la otra,
pero desasiéndose de sí también
cada cual
en su dorada, fecunda negligencia.

En su ritmo me despliego.
En su metrónomo
                caprichoso y fugaz
despliega el universo sus fantasmagorías
—su verdad.

No hay traducción posible.
—o sí la hay:
de lo uno a sí mismo,

XV.

The poem is the face in the mirror
more true than the face and mirror.
The poem is the flow of blood
                         beyond the body,
the rhythm of blood beyond blood
—its rigorous channels, its muffled and unitary beating.

The poem is the rhythm of the other in me
beyond me, always, beyond,
where my silence comes up against your rhythm
and reverberates in me, that I sol-fa in the poem
a numinous rhythm,
cipher that creates an echo in the echo
that is true body
—the numinous in you and me—
the cycle of the spheres touching and abandoning each other
—getting further away, yes, one from the other,
but also unbinding itself of itself
each one
in its golden, fecund negligence.

In its rhythm I unfold myself.
In its metronome
               capricious and fleeting
the universe unfolds its hallucinations
—its truth.

There is no possible translation.
—or perhaps there is:
of the one to oneself,

de lo uno a aquello que tantea y vence
de lo que sabe de sí
—su pobre imperio.

El poema, digo,
digo la música, digo   el movimiento
de la danza en el cuerpo, el de la piedra esculpida...
Y la música en el trazo y en la piedra, digo,
y el movimiento sinuoso y firme del poema,
docta cadencia, felicísima caída en el cruce
de todos los sentidos.

of the one to what blindly searches and triumphs
of what it knows of itself
—its poor empire.

The poem, I say,
I say the music, I say   the movement
of dance in the body, the one of sculpted stone…
And the music in the stroke and in the stone, I say,
and the poem's steady and sinuous movement,
learned cadence, the happiest fall in the crossing
of all senses.

XVI.

De muy lejos venimos
de muy lejos
el carcaj de lejanías lleno
poblado
de sombras luminosas
hitos
      para entender
      para seguir
      para seguir buscando
      para seguir errando y regresar

oh entusiasmo
sonora arquitectura
de encendidos vitrales

música es
la vida luminosa

XVI.

We come from so far away
from so far
the quiver of distances full
populated
by luminous shadows
landmarks
        to understand
        to go on
        to go on searching
        to go on erring and return

oh enthusiasm
sonorous architecture
of stained glass on fire

music is
the luminous life

XVII.

Pasan en naves los días
hacia vaya a saber qué ribera

Disolución
      Disolución

Nada
    Nada
        se diluye

                      —Por lo demás,
                          no hay ribera

:

un drama de máscaras vagantes
allí donde la voz es reina
y reina
    una música esculpida
en agua y piedra

En naves
      como alas
de palomas
          pasan
                extendidas

XVII.

The days pass in ships
toward who knows what shore

Dissolution
       Dissolution

Nothing
      Nothing
           is diluted

                                            —Otherwise,
                                          there is no shore

:

a theater of wandering masks
where the voice reigns
      and music sculpted
in water and stone
reigns

In ships
      like wings
of doves
          they pass
                    spread

Vaya a saber qué festín de sentidos
                       de vacíos
          de impronunciable
certitud
celebran
       allá tan hondo
en la anchurosa etérea a-
dormilada valseosa
nauseada
       blanca esfera del mar

vaivén de sombras
                vaivén
de tierras reveladas

Alguien pide volver
Volver
    al fondo y renacer

                                  ¿Qué se querrá?

En naves pasan los días
Rojo   Verde   Azul...
Flamean
      asidos a las velas
como pálidos brazos púberes ondeando
a ras del horizonte

Who knows what a banquet of senses
              of emptinesses
         of unpronounceable
certainty
they celebrate
         so deep
in the wide ethereal s-
leepy walzing
nauseated
         white sphere of the sea

undulation of shadows
                    undulation
of lands revealed

Someone asks to return
Return
     to the bottom and be reborn

                              What could they want?

In ships the days pass
Red   Green   Blue…
They blaze
          clinging to the sails
like pale nubile arms waving
level with the horizon

                                        ¿Qué se querrá?

Se eleva
una canción
    honda
        jonda
            umbría
        elemental

Pasan los días
        bogando
por un río de esbeltas algas
cimbreando
a ras del cielo

                                    What could they want?

A song
comes forth
          deep
              soulful
                    umber
                  elemental

The days pass
              rowing
down a river of svelte algae
swaying
level with the sky

XVIII.

—*Cuando estábamos a punto de salir de la abertura, después de haber cumplido el castigo señalado a nuestras culpas, vimos a Ardieo entre muchos otros, tiranos en su mayoría, aunque no faltaban algunos particulares que habían cometido grandes delitos. Unos hombres salvajes y ardientes, apostados junto a la abertura, al oír el rugido les interceptaban el paso, obligándolos a retroceder, y a Ardieo y a los demás les ataron los pies, las manos y el cuello, y después de arrojarlos en tierra y desollarlos, los arrastraron fuera del camino, desgarrándolos contra las zarzas espinosas...*

(Rep., X)

(—De un modo u otro...
asegurémonos primero
alguna sanción aquí.)

XVIII.

—*As we were about to leave through the cavern's entrance, after having undergone the punishment assigned to each of our sins, we saw Ardiaeus among many, mostly tyrants, although there were plenty of those who had committed other great crimes.*

Savage men on fire, standing near the entrance, upon hearing the bellowing, impeded their progress, forcing them to go back, and they tied the feat, hands, and necks of Ardiaeus and the others, and after hurling them through the dirt and flaying them, they dragged them from the path, tearing them against the thorny brambles...

(Rep., X)

(—In one way or another...
let us first ensure
a sanction here.)

XIX.

Dime que tú lo has visto
Dime que tú también
que sabes
que en eso, al menos
—lo último-primordial—
somos hermanos

Tú en la guerra
Tú en la miseria
Tú, apedreador
Tú, constructor de casas
Tú que insistes en que busquen tu nombre
                             en el registro de lo humano
Tú que buscas o finges que buscas un nombre que no encuentras

Tú que sabes que te humillan hasta cuando pronuncian tu nombre

Dime que la gracia
                     al menos
no nos separa

XIX.

Tell me you have seen it
Tell me that you as well
that you know
that in this, at least
—the ultimate-primordial—
we are kin

You in war
You in misery
You, who stone others
You, builder of houses
You who insist your name be searched
                           in the human registry
You who search or pretend to search for a name you do not find

You who know they humiliate you even when they pronounce your
                                                        name

Tell me that grace
                at least
does not divide us

XX.

Caída no hubo.
Lo alto está aquí. Es aquí.
Adentro.

Caída no hubo.
Distracciones hay. Vientos. Fugas.
Maquinarias. Grandes, grandes.
Juegos de sombra, preocupación y olvido. De sí.
Siempre los hubo.

Cada época. Cada
civilización
retratada en su propio engranaje
de humillaciones y olvido. De sí.
Robar el fuego no es robar ni es fuego.
Recordar es remontarse, preservar para sí el acceso
al resplandor custodiado por
    —no sus guardianes, sino sus enemigos.
Vertedero de sombra y sangre.
Cuanto mayor pobreza, más olvido.
Cuanta más prepotencia, menos luz.

En sí y fuera de sí
—todo es uno—
sola morada de pura geometría
y luz rigiendo
mansa, inexorablemente, generosa-
mente bañando
todo de sí.

XX.

There was no fall.
The summit is here. It is here.
Inside.

There was no fall.
There are distractions. Winds. Fugues.
Machineries. Huge, huge.
Plays of shadows, worry and oblivion. Of oneself.
There always was.

Each epoch. Each
civilization
pictured in its own apparatus
of humiliations and oblivion. Of itself.
To thieve the fire is not to thieve nor is it fire.
To remember is to soar, preserve for oneself the access
to the resplendence guarded
            —not by its keeper, but its enemies.
Dump heap of shadow and blood.
The more poverty, the more oblivion.
The more brute arrogance, the less light.

In and out of itself
—all is one—
single abode of pure geometry
and light that governs
docile, inexorably, generous-
ly bathing
all of itself.

Luz estético-ética.
Olvidada de sí —entregada.
Fórmula-Madre.

Y aun hay Algo. Algo, fuera
que no se piensa.

Otro tono. Otra
modulación de la luz.

Allá en origen.

Aesthetic-ethic light.
Oblivious of itself—given.
Formula-Mother.

And there is still Something. Something, outside
that is not thought.

Another tone. Another
modulation of light.

There at the beginning.

Epílogo

Epilogue

"—¿Me quieres?
Dime que me quieres.
Dime mil veces al día
que me quieres."

En el origen fue el Bien.
Y de él, todas las cosas.

"—Do you love me?
Tell me you love me.
Tell me a thousand times a day
you love me."

*In the beginning there was Goodness.
And from it, all things.*

MERCEDES ROFFÉ (Buenos Aires, 1954) is one of Argentina's most important and internationally recognized contemporary poets. Her works include *Poemas* (1977), *El tapiz* (published under the heteronym, Ferdinand Oziel, 1983), *Cámara baja* (1987; 1996), *La noche y las palabras* (1996; 1998), *Definiciones Mayas* (1999), *Antología poética* (2000), *Canto errante* (2002), *Memorial de agravios* (2002), *La ópera fantasma* (2005; 2012), *Las linternas flotantes* (2009) and the volume of selected works, *Milenios caen de su vuelo* (2005). *Mansión nocturna*, a second volume of collected works, is forthcoming from Monte Ávila in 2015. Among other distinctions, Roffé was awarded a John Simon Guggenheim Memorial Fellowship in poetry (2001) and, more recently, a Civitella Ranieri Foundation Center residency fellowship (2012). Roffé lives in New York City and is the founding director of Ediciones Pen Press.

ANNA DEENY MORALES has translated poetry by Raúl Zurita, Mercedes Roffé, Alejandra Pizarnik, Amanda Berenguer, Nicanor Parra, Gabriela Mistral, Idea Vilariño, Marosa di Giorgio and Malú Urriola. She is the editor and translator of *Sky Below*, a volume of selected works by Zurita, forthcoming from Northwestern University Press. She has a PhD from the University of California, Berkeley, and teaches at the Center for Latin American Studies at Georgetown University. Deeny is currently writing a book about sound, poetry and translation.

www.ingramcontent.com/pod-product-compliance
Lightning Source LLC
Chambersburg PA
CBHW031200160426
43193CB00008B/452